The ABC's of Origami

PAPER FOLDING FOR CHILDREN

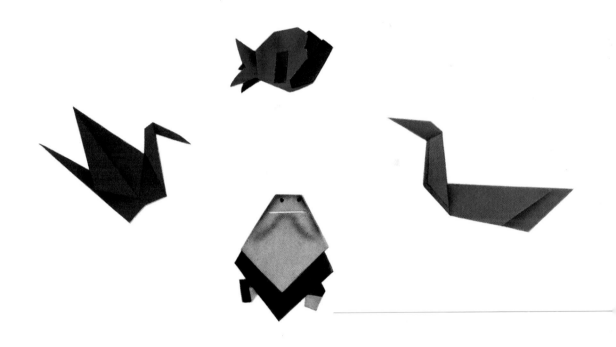

by CLAUDE SARASAS

ILLUSTRATED BY THE AUTHOR

CHARLES E. TUTTLE COMPANY, INC.
Rutland, Vermont & Tokyo, Japan.

*Published by the Charles E Tuttle Company, Inc
of Rutland, Vermont & Tokyo, Japan
with editorial offices at
Suido 1-chome, 2-6, Bunkyo-ku, Tokyo, Japan*

© *1964, by Charles E. Tuttle Co , Inc
All Rights Reserved*

*Library of Congress Catalog Card No. 64-17160
International Standard Book No. 0-8048-0000-6*

*First printing, 1964
Twenty-sixth printing, 1996*

Introduction

WHAT a wonderful thing is a square of paper! With a few folds here and there, it becomes a boat, an Indian wigwam, a nesting bird, Santa Claus, or nearly anything else you can name. Easy? Yes. Fun? You bet.

Educational, too. Through origami—paper folding—Japanese children learn to use their hands and develop their creative abilities. In the United States and in other countries, more and more teachers and nurses are using origami with their students and patients.

As a hobby, origami offers creative adventures for grownups as well as youngsters. I know engineers, musicians, housewives, businessmen, and others who find endless fun and relaxation in this Japanese art. Lewis Carroll was an ardent paper folder; so were Leonardo da Vinci and Harry Houdini.

For learning the ABC's of paper folding, I know of no book so delightful and instructive as Claude Sarasas' *The ABC's of Origami.* The earlier edition, of which only a few expensive copies were printed, is today regarded as a collector's item. Now, thanks to Charles E. Tuttle, this beautiful classic is available to us all.

Mrs. Sarasas' charming illustrations are but one reason why this is my favorite origami book. A better reason is her step-by-step diagrams, which are unusually clear. Take your time, follow each step carefully, and the world of origami is yours.

And a wonderful world it is.

Lillian Oppenheimer
Director, The Origami Center
New York City

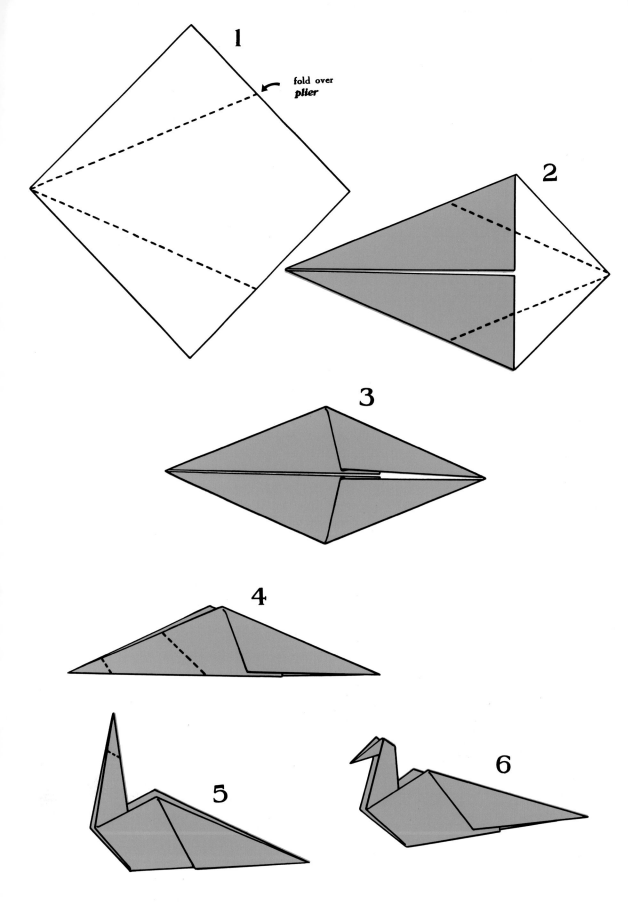

1

fold over
plier

2

3

4

5

6

4

 # ALBATROSS
ALBATROS
AHŌDORI

あほうどり　（信天翁）

1

2

3

4

5

6

turn over
tourner

7

6

BOAT
BATEAU
FUNE

ふね　　　（舟）

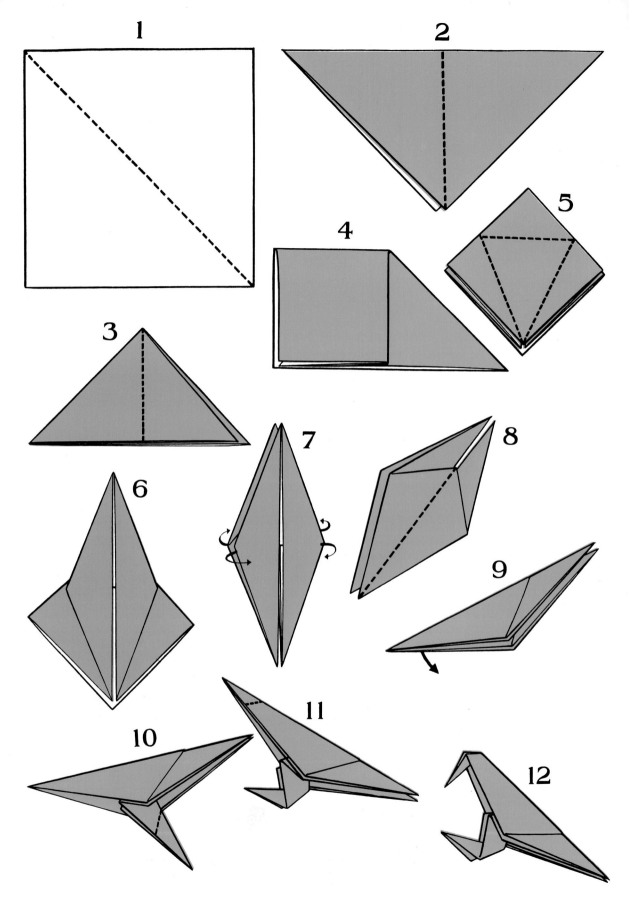

C CROW
CORBEAU
KARASU

か　ら　す　（鴉）

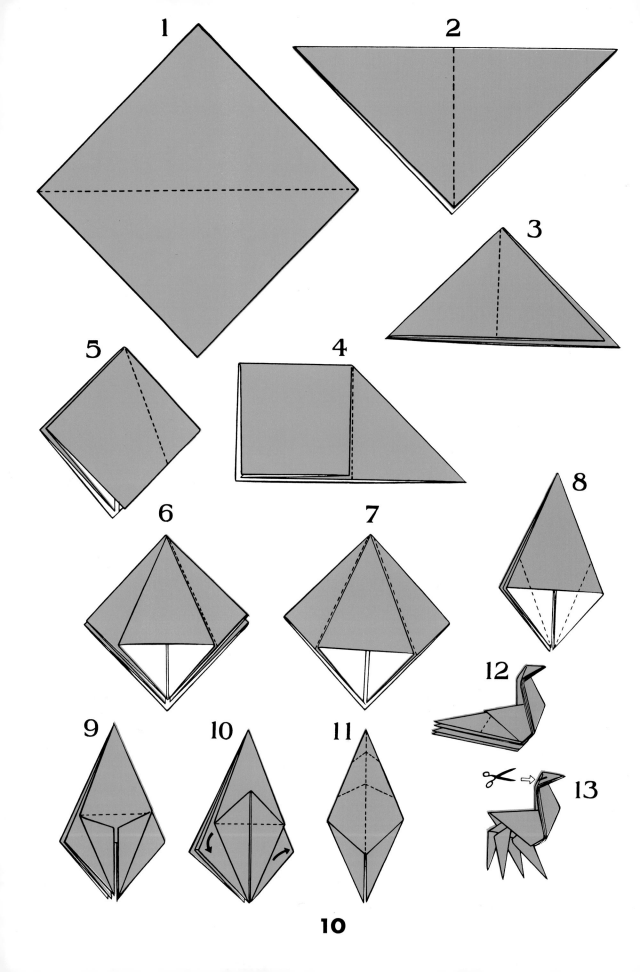

10

DEER
DAIM
SHIKA

しか　　　　（鹿）

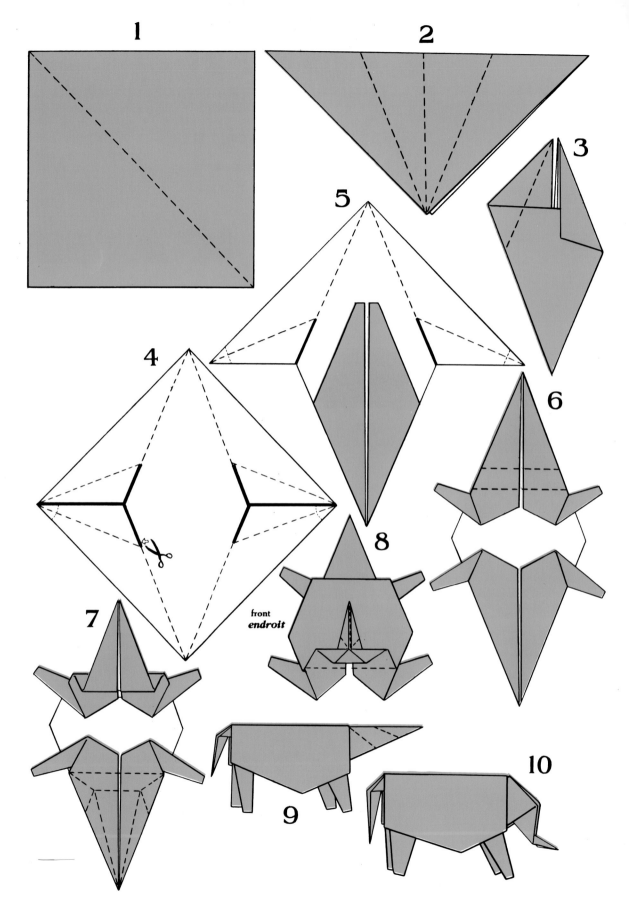

1

2

3

5

4

6

8

front
endroit

7

9

10

E

ELEPHANT
ELÉPHANT
Zō

ぞ　う　　　（象）

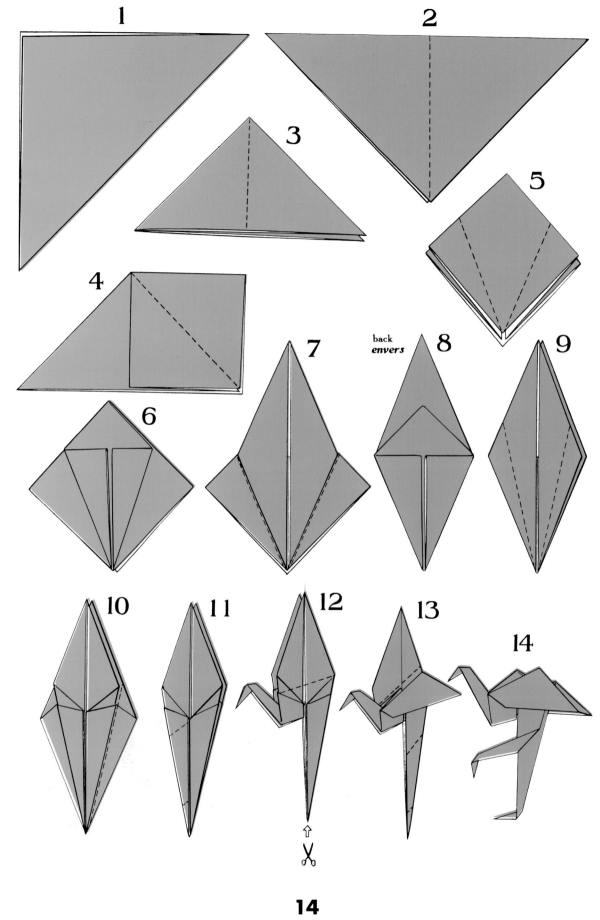

1

2

3

4

5

6

7

back
envers

8

9

10

11

12

13

14

14

F

FLAMINGO
FLAMANT
BENIZURU

べ に づ る 　　（紅鶴）

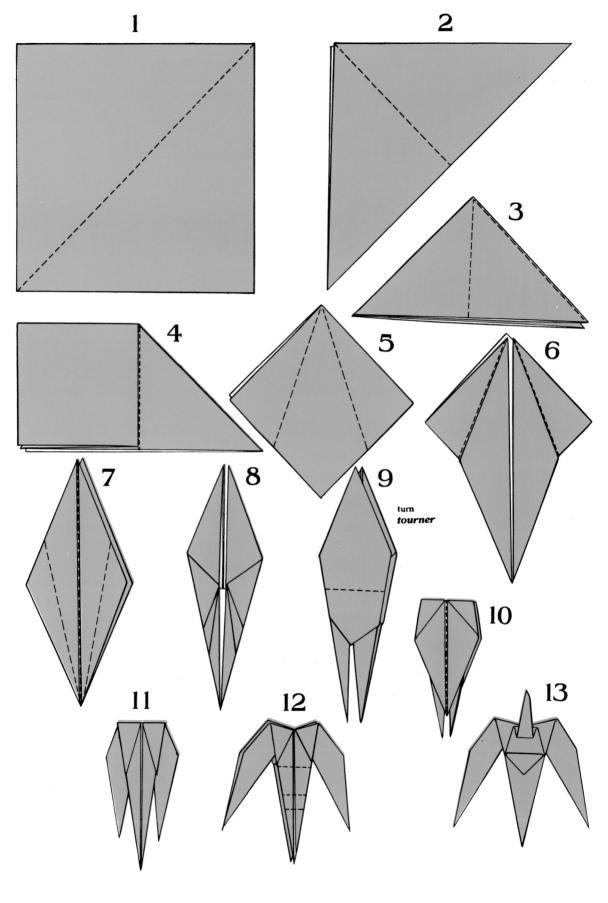

turn
tourner

16

GULL
GOÉLAND
KAMOME

かもめ （鷗）

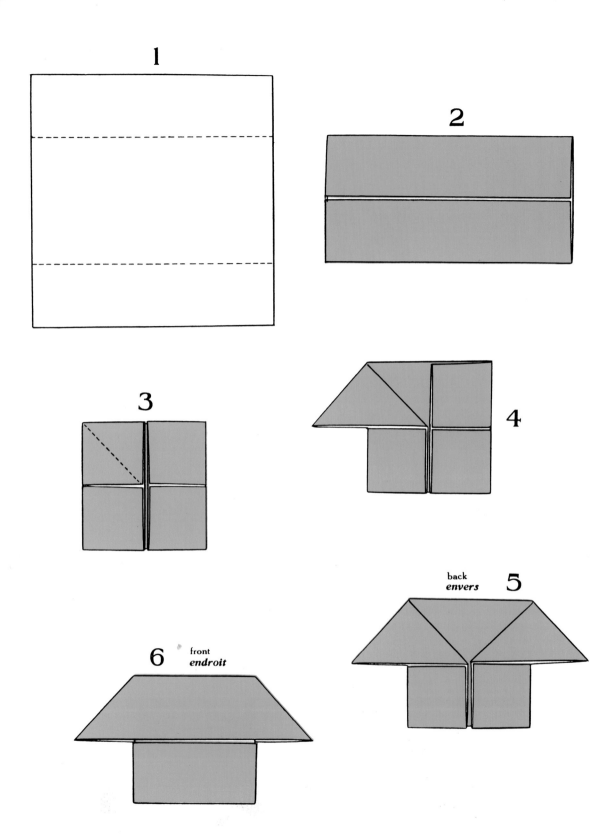

1

2

3

4

back
envers 5

front
endroit 6

18

H HUT HUTTE KOYA

こや　　　　（小屋）

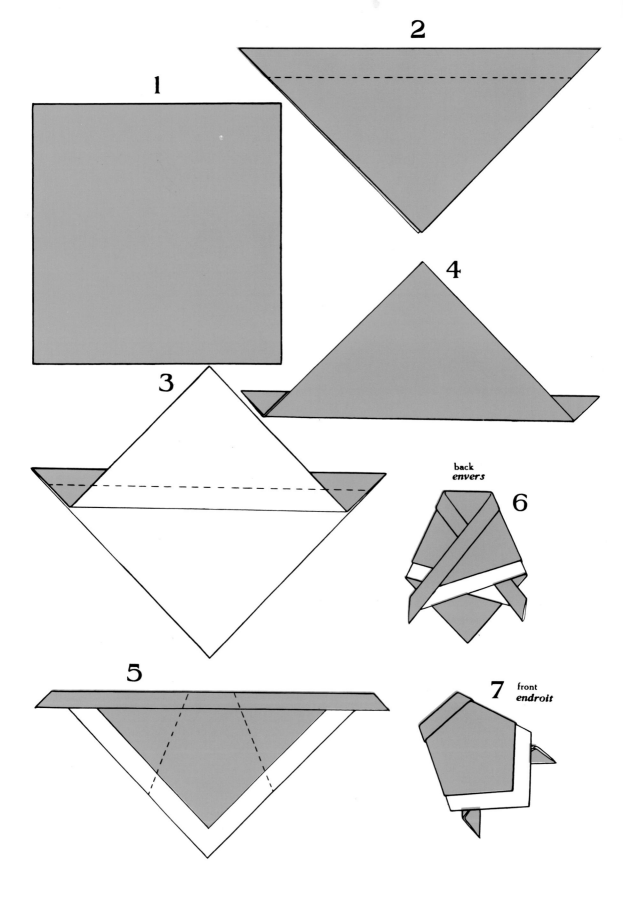

1

2

3

4

5

6
back
envers

7
front
endroit

I INSECT
INSECTE
MUSHI

むし　　　（虫）

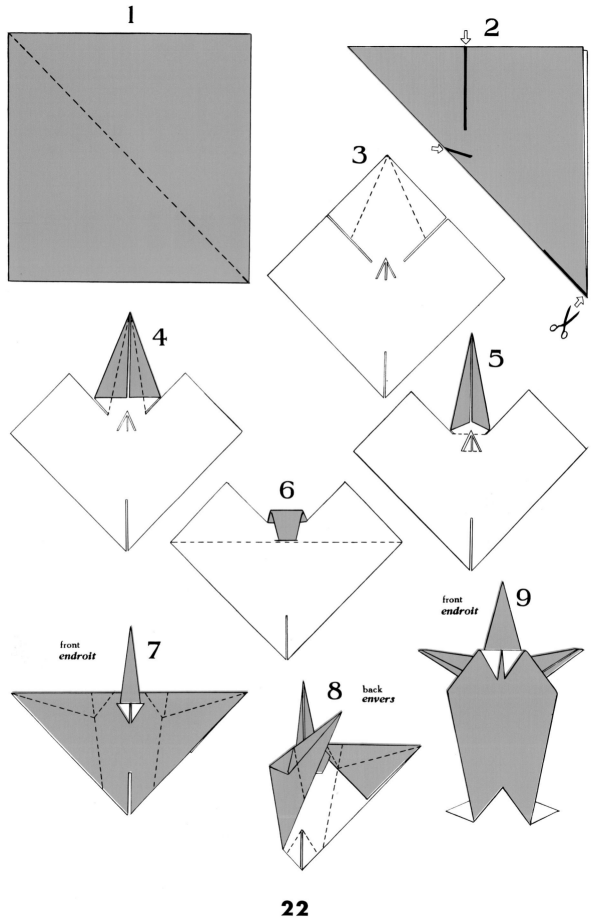

1

2

3

4

5

6

7

front
endroit

8

back
envers

front
endroit

9

22

JUGGLER
JONGLEUR
TEJINASHI

てじなし （手品師）

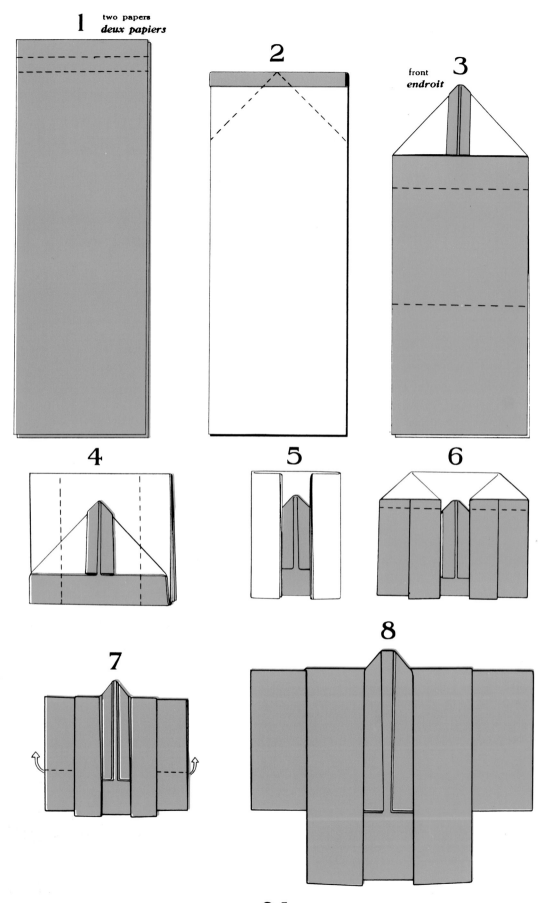

1 two papers *deux papiers*

2

3 front *endroit*

4

5

6

7

8

24

K KIMONO KIMONO KIMONO

きもの （着物）

1

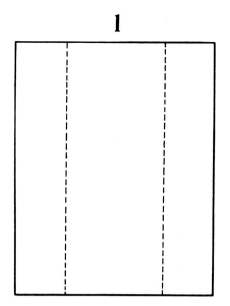

2

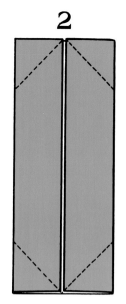

3

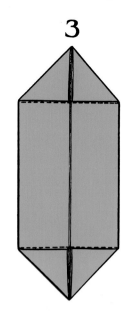

4

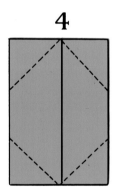

5

front
endroit

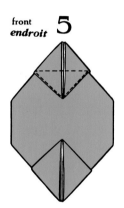

6

back
envers

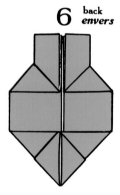

7

front
endroit

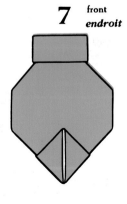

8

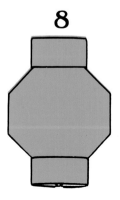

26

L

LANTERN
LANTERNE
CHÔCHIN

ちょうちん　　（提燈）

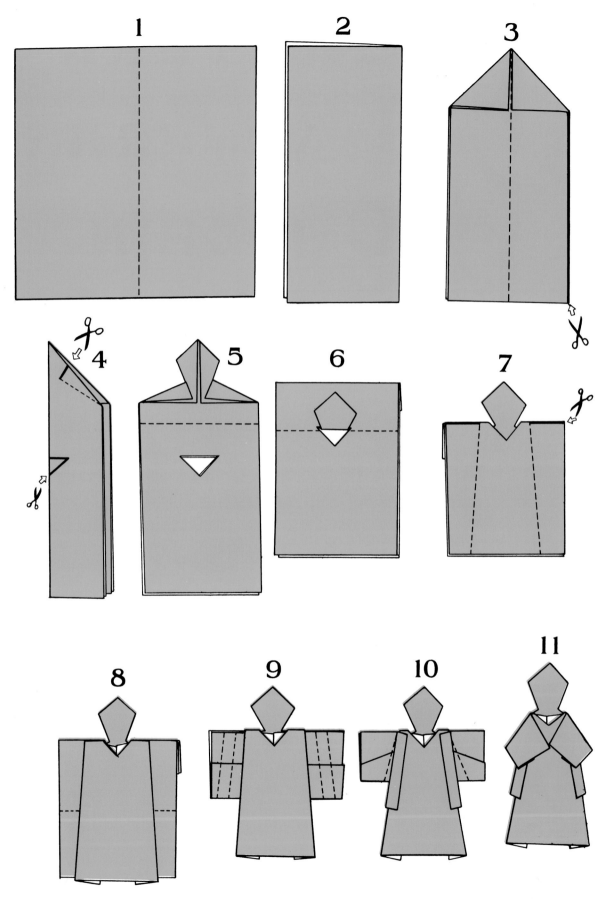

1
2
3
4
5
6
7
8
9
10
11

M MANDARIN
MANDARIN
MIYABITO

みやびと　　（宮人）

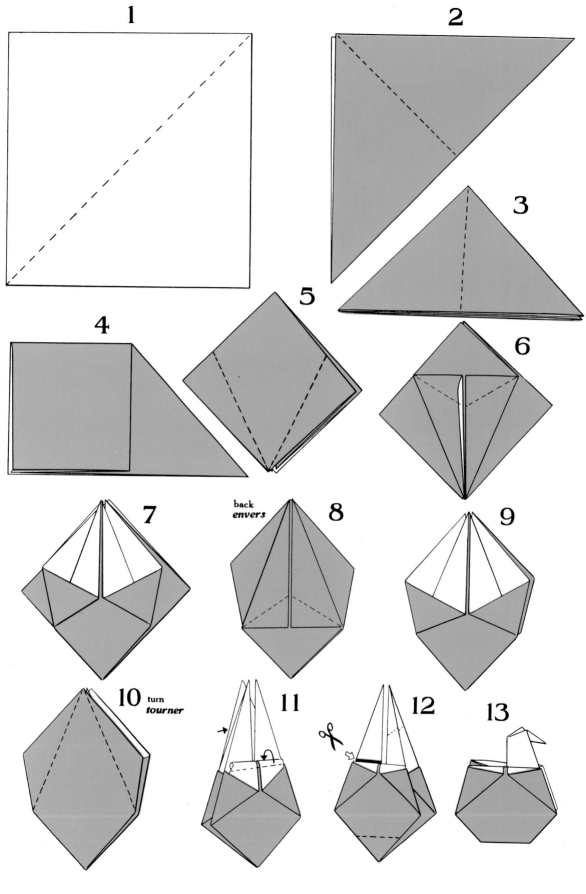

1

2

3

4

5

6

7

back
envers

8

9

10 turn
tourner

11

12

13

30

N

NEST
NID
SU

す　　（巣）

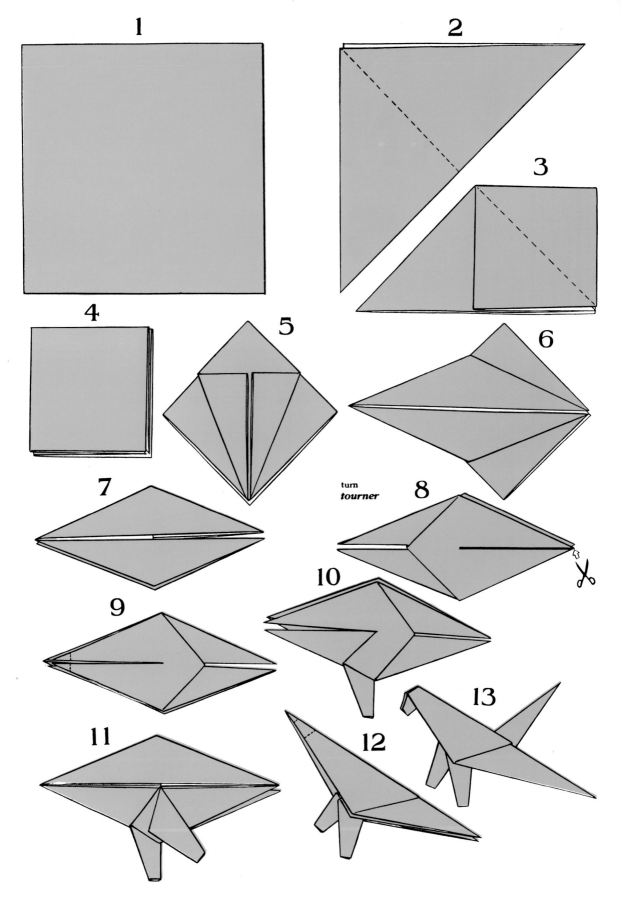

1

2

3

4

5

6

7

turn
tourner

8

9

10

11

12

13

OTARIID
OTARIE
ASHIKA

あしか（海驢）

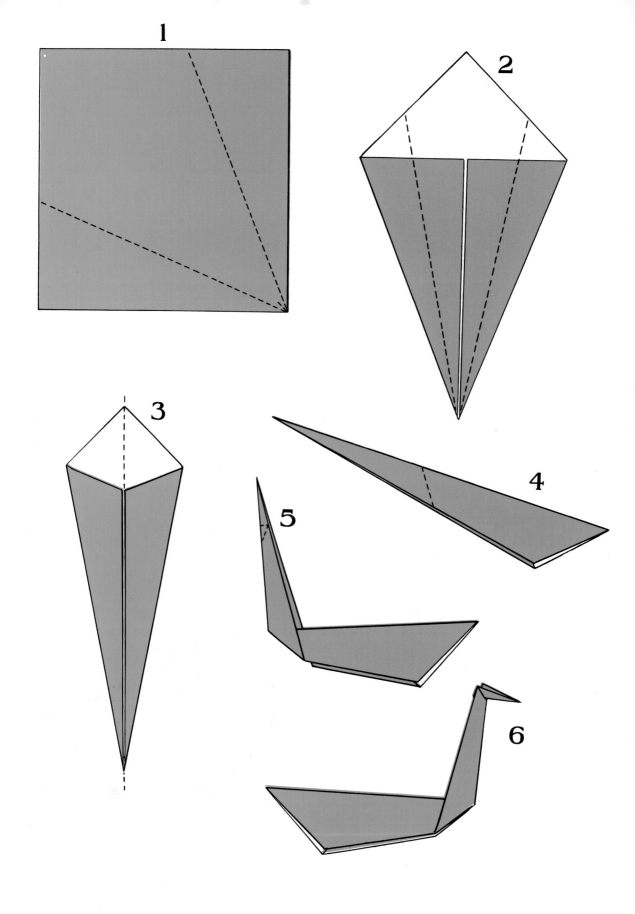

P PEACOCK PAON KUJAKU

くじゃく　　（孔雀）

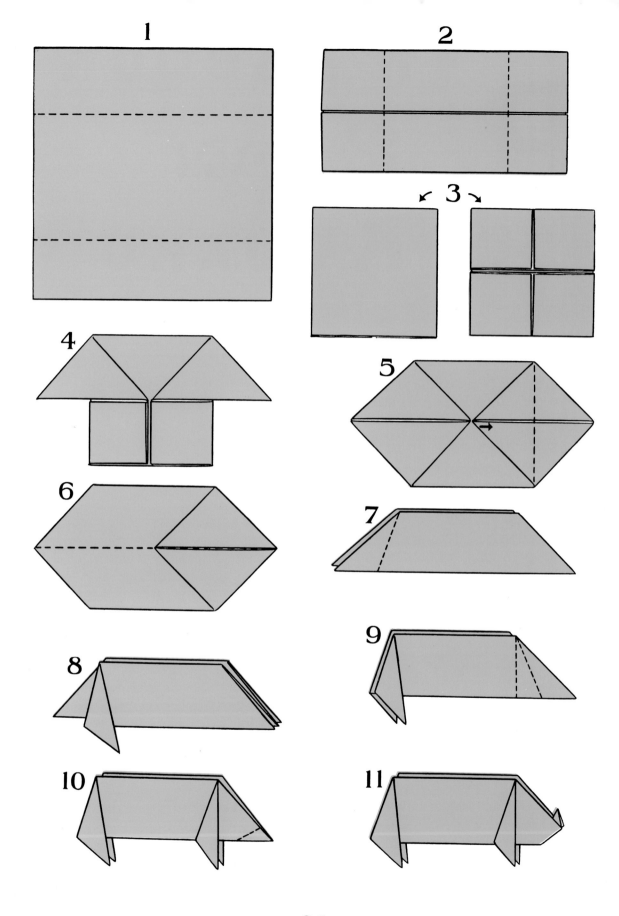

QUADRUPED

QUADRUPÈDE

KEMONO

けもの （獣類）

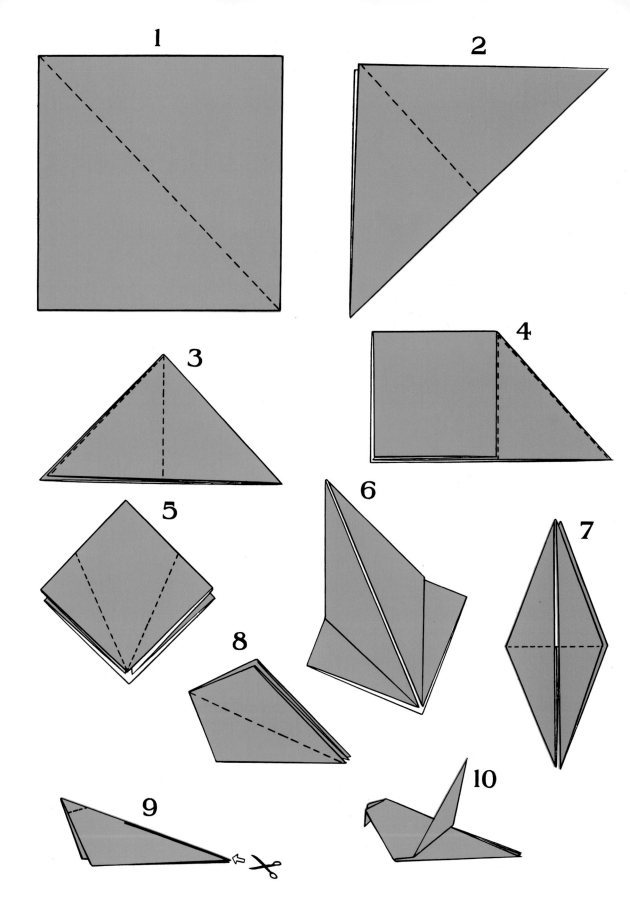

ROBIN
ROUGE-GORGE:
KOMADORI

こまどり 　　（駒鳥）

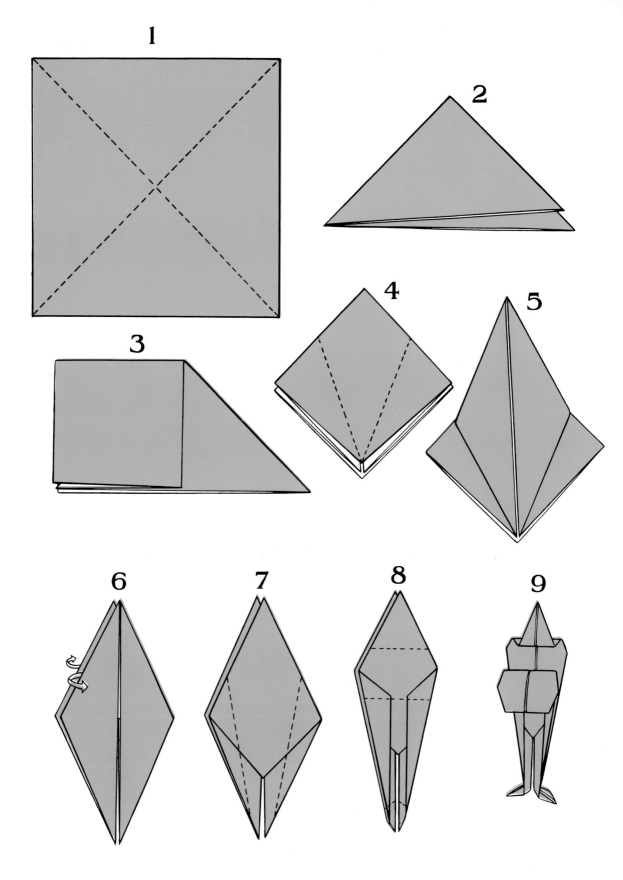

SANTA CLAUS
SAINT NICOLAS
SANTA KURŌSU

さんたくろーす

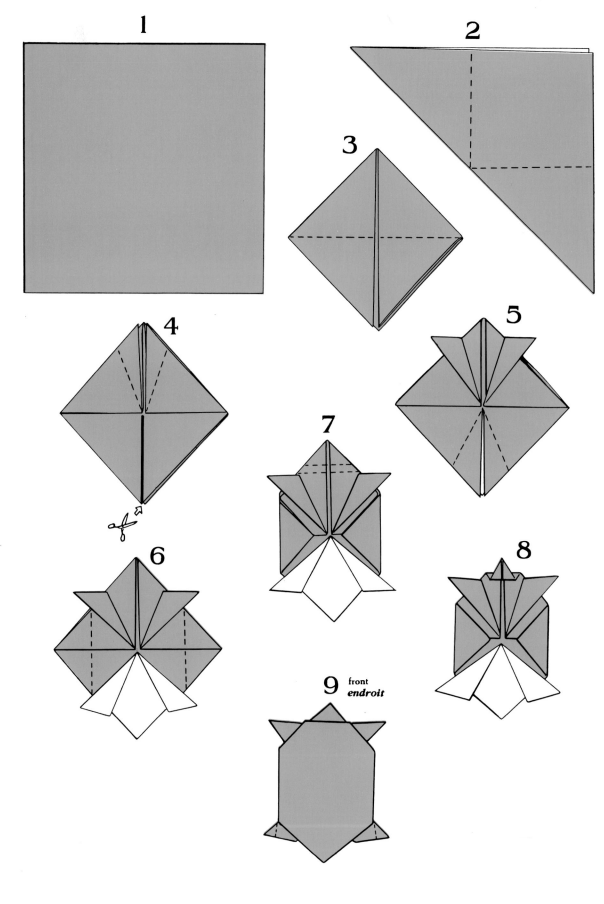

1

2

3

4

5

6

7

8

9 front
endroit

42

TORTOISE
TORTUE
KAME

かめ　（龜）

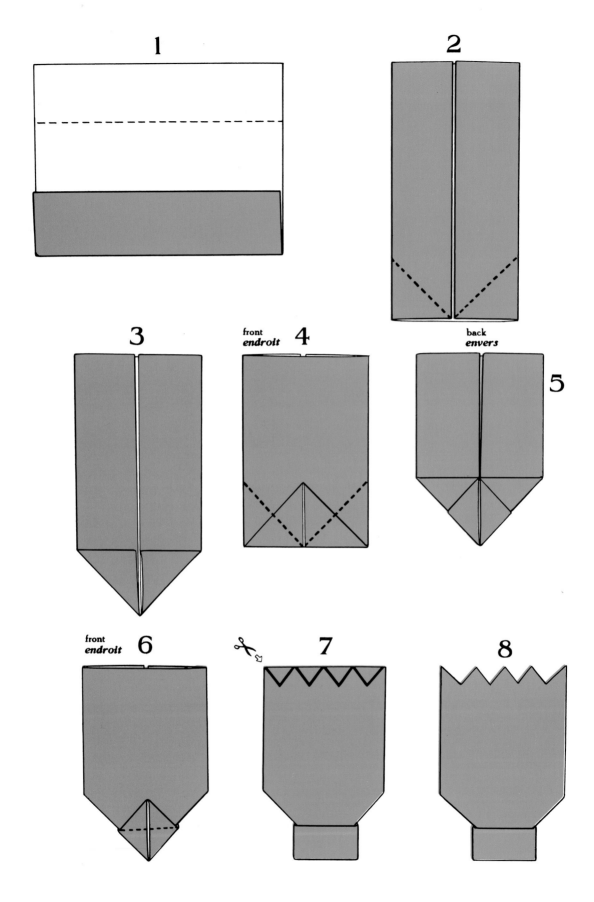

1

2

3

4
front
endroit

back
envers

5

6
front
endroit

7

8

44

U URN
URNE:
TSUBO

つぼ 　　（壺）

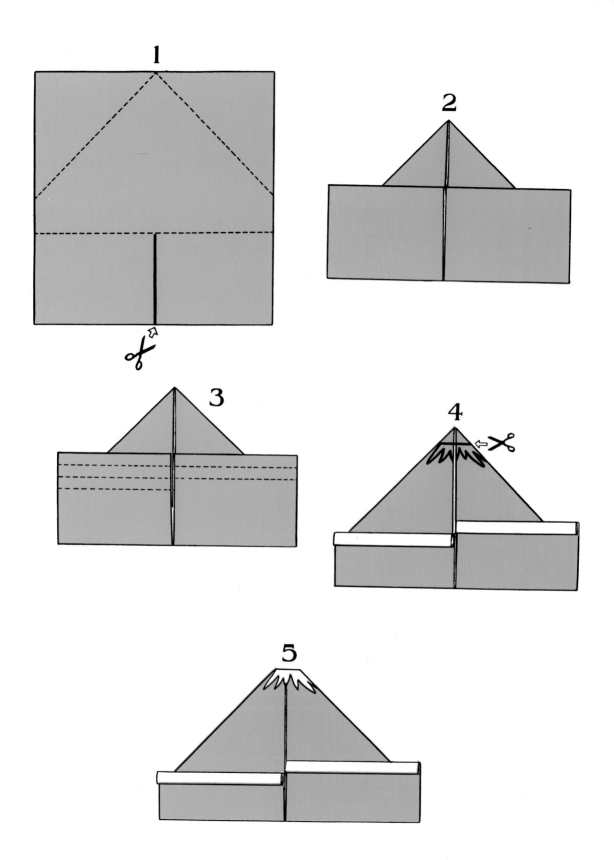

VOLCANO
VOLCAN
FUNKAZAN

ふんかざん （噴火山）

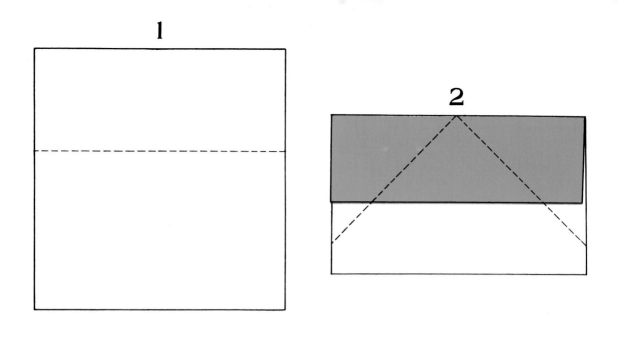

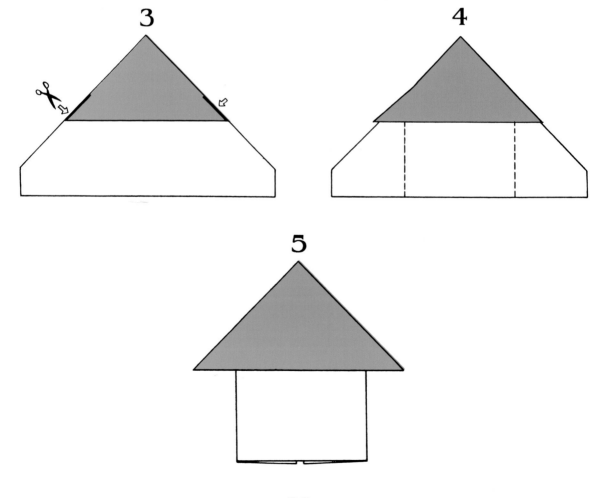

48

Wigwam
Wigwam
Bakusha

ばくしや　　（幕舎）

49

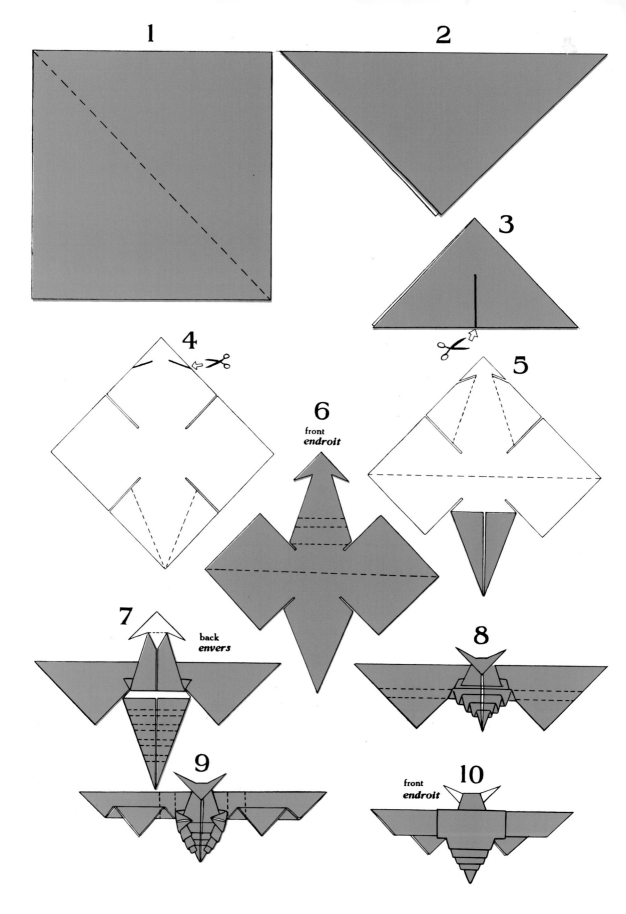

1

2

3

4

5

6
front
endroit

7
back
envers

8

9

10
front
endroit

XANTHIA
XANTIE
KIGIKU

きぎく（黄菊）

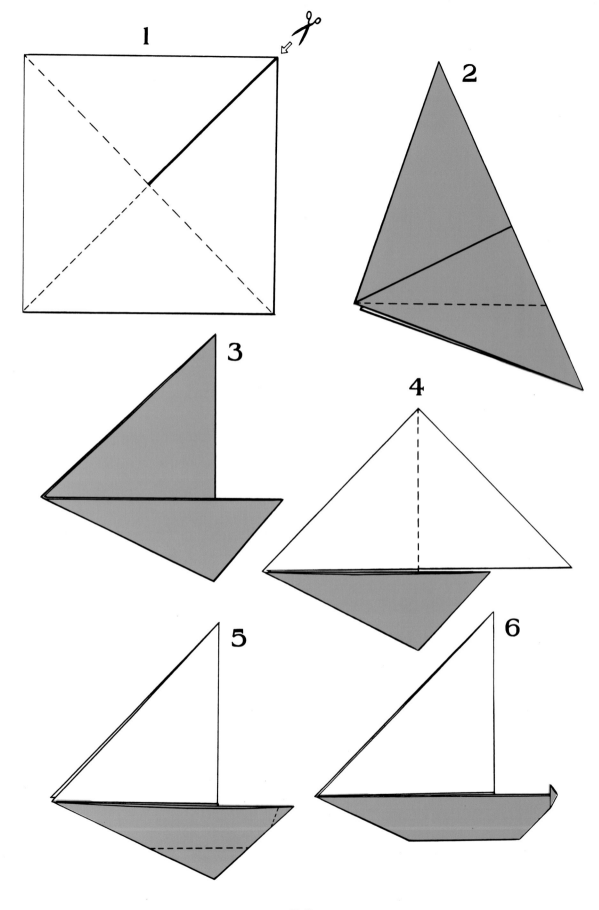

YACHT
YACHT
YOTTO

よ つ と （帆船）

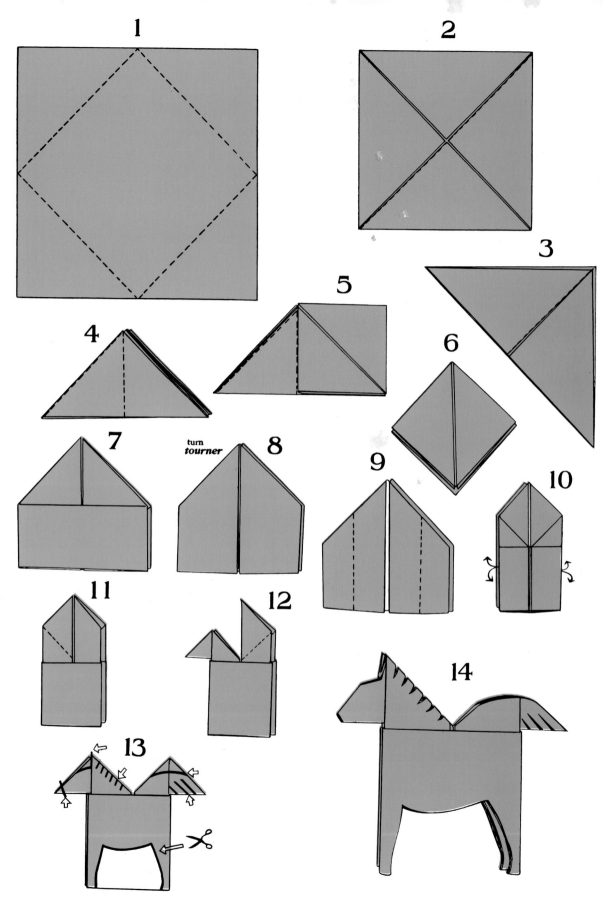

1

2

3

4

5

6

7

turn
tourner

8

9

10

11

12

13

14

54

Z ZEBRA
ZÈBRE
SHIMAUMA

しまうま　　（縞馬）

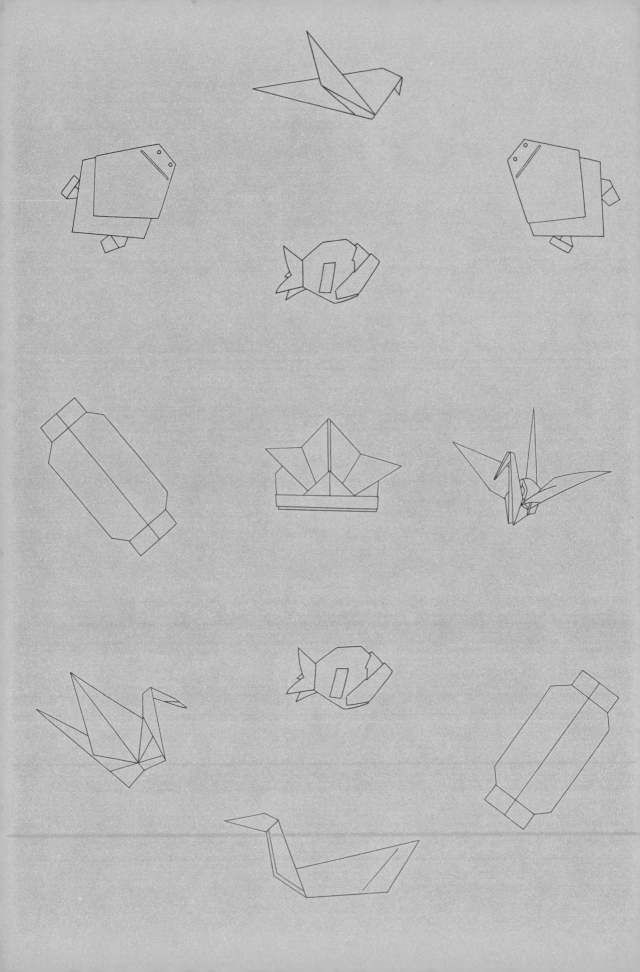